VIDEO BLOG(

I0021886

Make Money Online through vlogging on YouTube and other video web marketing platforms

BOOK DESCRIPTION

Video marketing has become more prominent as more people join the internet world. Video content has become one of the leading sources of traffic as people become more inclined to watch videos than to read blogs. Thus, it is important to recognize your real and potential customers' perceptions and act accordingly. Video marketing is the greatest thing you can do to serve this increasing consumer preference towards video content.

This book introduces you to the world of vlogging. It endeavors to show you how to leverage vlogging with video marketing so that you can optimize on your marketing campaign. It goes further to provide you with critical information that lets you compare video marketing with other forms of marketing to make an informed and assured decision.

Videos, just as blog posts, and websites, need to be hosted. There are plenty of video hosting platforms that you can use. However, not all are the same. Some are more inclined towards hosting artistic videos while others are more inclined to hosting social videos. You should be able to choose a platform that fits well into your marketing strategy. This book guides you through the various video marketing platforms and provides you with crucial information that will help you choose the best hosting platform for your marketing videos.

Hosting your videos is one thing. Effectively using your videos to market your products and services is another thing altogether. This book adequately guides you on how to use your videos effectively to optimize your marketing strategy, achieve higher conversion rates and boost sales.

Affiliate marketing is no doubt one of the best ways to market your products without incurring huge overhead costs in terms of money, time and effort. It is the most preferred way of marketing on the internet by small-scale businesses and startups. Even large-scale businesses such as Amazon have embraced affiliate marketing to expand, widen and intensify their reach. You too can take advantage of affiliate marketing. However, video affiliate marketing requires a slightly different approach compared to the traditional text-based affiliate marketing. In this book, you will learn how to strategically create affiliate-marketing videos and optimize them for higher conversion.

Though vlogging is gaining a lot of web territory, blogging is still far from being dislodged. The good thing is that you can blend both for maximum effect. You can drive traffic to your video channel using blogs. More importantly, you can also use videos to drive traffic to your landing page and product page. Thus, they are not substitutes but complementary. In this book, you will be guided on how to blog with video marketing to gain an optimum outcome.

Finally, social media cannot be ignored when it comes to video marketing. The greatest advantage of social media is that it can make your content go viral. Virality is a great gain to your marketing endeavor. Yet, not all videos go viral. You must specifically prepare for it. This book guides you on the critical ingredients of a viral video. It also guides you on how to make a viral video. More importantly, it shows you how to trigger the virality.

Keep reading!

ABOUT THE AUTHOR

George Pain is an entrepreneur, author and business consultant. He specializes in setting up online businesses from scratch, investment income strategies and global mobility solutions. He has successfully built several businesses from the ground up and is excited to share his knowledge with you.

DISCLAIMER

CONTENTS

VIDEO BLOGGING 1

BOOK DESCRIPTION 2

ABOUT THE AUTHOR 5

DISCLAIMER 6

CONTENTS.. 7

INTRODUCTION 9

WHAT IS VLOGGING? 10

HOW DOES VIDEO MARKETING COMPARE WITH OTHER FORMS OF MARKETING? 16

DIFFERENT VIDEO MARKETING PLATFORMS....................24

USING VIDEOS TO MARKET YOUR PRODUCTS 35

DRIVING TRAFFIC TO YOUR WEBSITES WITH VIDEOS.......44

AFFILIATE MARKETING WITH VIDEO MARKETING............49

BLOGGING WITH VIDEO MARKETING 54

INCREASE YOUR CHANCES OF MAKING VIRAL VIDEO 60

OTHER WAYS TO USE VIDEO MARKETING 67

CONCLUSION 70

INTRODUCTION

Video content has already surpassed both text-based and image-based content in terms of generating web traffic. In fact, video content generates almost two-thirds of the web traffic today and it is projected to generate 80% of web traffic by the year 2019. Like any other shrewd businessperson, you know that where there is huge traffic there is a greater customer potential. The same applies to videos.

Video marketing has become a compelling necessity as more consumers show higher affinity for video content. You have to feed them what they want in a profitable manner. This book guides you on how to sharpen your brand visibility, boost customer loyalty and increase sales using videos.

Do not be left out. Be part of the video marketing revolution. Propel your business through video marketing. Let this book show you how.

Enjoy reading!

WHAT IS VLOGGING?

The internet revolution has come with its own rich terminology. This has enabled internet users to communicate in a language that they can easily understand. Vlogging is a popular terminology. However, some are still yet to understand its meaning. In this section, we will not only explore what it is but also go further to understand why it is necessary to do it, and how to do it.

Meaning of Vlogging

Vlogging refers to the use of videos for the purposes of blogging. It is a refined form of blogging where 'v' has replaced 'b' to emphasize that video takes the core essence as opposed to text. Thus, instead of talking of a blog as in blogging, we talk of 'vlog' as in vlogging. In addition, instead of the blogosphere, we have vlogosphere; and, instead of bloggers, we have vloggers. A vlog is simply a post whose content is mainly in form of video. A vlog can have text, but not necessarily.

Prior to the internet community settling on 'vlog', other common terms were 'podcast', 'videocast', or 'vodcast'. What makes a vlog unique is that it is a first-person, self-made video. The podcast is still being commonly used, though, mainly refers audio.

How has vlogging shaped digital content consumption?

According to eMarketer, vlog viewers have grown by almost 87% from 372 million in 2012 to 700 million by 2016. Time spent viewing vlogs has also risen dramatically within the same period by 120% from the original 26 minutes to about 1 hour. On the other hand, mobile video viewing has grown by 367% within the same period.

The demand for vlogs has created more entrants such as Snapchat, Facebook Live, Vine, Periscope, and Instagram. In fact, as of now, most social network platforms have vlogs natively provided. The advent of the smartphone brought this huge surge in demand for vlogs and thus the rise of micro-vlogging sites such as Snapchat.

The rise of vlogs has also propelled the rise of popular vloggers who have become great influencers in their own regard. Influential vloggers have hundreds of times more followers than influential bloggers. This has attracted the attention of marketers as brands continue to see vlog influencers as the best way to break through the ad clutter and have a competitive advantage. Vloggers are capable of swaying attitudes of their audiences and thus make their followers more receptive to the products that they are endorsing.

Why is Vlogging becoming so popular?

The following are main reasons for vlogging's popularity:

- **More improved and cheaper facility** – Hardware required for vlogging has become increasingly cheaper over time. They have also greatly improved their performance. We do have more powerful desktops and smartphones at a cheaper price. This makes it possible to store larger volumes of videos, process them faster and streamline them. The Internet has also become faster (with the widespread of fiber cables), cheaper and more available. This has enabled High Definition (HD) video content to be streamed on not only desktops but also more so on smartphones.

- **Viewers' preferences** – Generally, video content is easier to capture and consolidate in the memory than text content. Thus, viewers prefer video content that they could consume faster and easier.

- **More content** – A vlog can package more content/message within the same duration than a blog. For example, it is hard for a blog to capture body language while a vlog will do. Communication experts allude that nearly 75% of communication we receive is from body language e.g. via a change of tone, hand gestures, facial expressions etc. This cannot be captured by a blog.

- **A great tool for business owners** – Business owners have also fallen in love with vlogs. This is because that is what attracts the attention their existing and potential customers the most. With over 1 billion people visiting YouTube every month, YouTube is the place for entrepreneurs to be. Furthermore, a vlog enables business owners to demonstrate product usage and product features with more ease than they could achieve with blogs. This greatly boosts consumer experience.
- **High credibility** – Vlogs are more credible as viewers can see the actual person as opposed to a blog where you can only rely on the person's name. This helps to build trust.

Why should you vlog?

If you are a digital marketer, then, vlogging is not an option but a compelling necessity. This is because the number of vlog viewers has already surpassed the number of blog readers and continues to grow as smartphones become more affordable and more powerful. Nevertheless, this is being complemented by increasingly faster internet and cheaper smartphones.

The following are some of the reasons why you ought to vlog as a marketer:

- **Vlogs are easy to digest** – Video content is received via multiple senses (visual and auditory). It is easier for the brain to digest the content and derive meaning. It is also easier for your memory to consolidate and retain the content. This makes video content one of the best ways for your brand to communicate with your audience. Video content is easier to understand, more engaging and highly interactive. This means that viewers will be more receptive to video ads. According to Hubspot, almost 75% of online video viewers have interacted with an online video ad. Furthermore, 92% of mobile users have shared video content.

- **Vlogs are affordable** – Vlogs are highly affordable. For a start, you only need a smartphone (for both audio and visual capture) or a webcam on a laptop/desktop with inbuilt microphone. This makes them ideal for small businesses and startups. Furthermore, you can maximize exposure of a video through multiple video channels, email addresses, social media, and other platforms (including TVs). You can then advance gradually as you involve more sophisticated video capture gadgets and video editing software.

- **Vlogs help you develop a rapport** – Vlogs are personalized. They help you develop a personal connection with your audience. This is extremely crucial for brand loyalty. You develop a brand voice for your products and thus spur a loyal following.

HOW DOES VIDEO MARKETING COMPARE WITH OTHER FORMS OF MARKETING?

Videos continue to gain the attention of digital marketers. This is so because of the increasing preference of netizens for video content. The consolidation of the dominant position of YouTube, quick rise of Snapchat and surprisingly successful entry of Instagram and Facebook Live have all provided a bold signal that this is the future of digital marketing.

Established findings

- Brain processing advantage – The human brain processes visuals (videos) sixty thousand times faster than text. This means that people will easily digest a vlog message than they would digest a blog message.
- Content advantage– 60 seconds of video is equivalent to 1.8 million words. This means that you can pack more in a video than you would in a text content or audio alone.
- Consumption advantage – It is estimated that within the last 30 days, more video has been consumed on the web than what has been consumed by TV for the last 30 years.

These findings clearly show the comparative advantage of video marketing over other forms of marketing.

Info Statistics

- Video traffic had already been projected to consume 69% of all internet traffic in 2017 and is projected to consume 80% of all internet traffic by 2019 (Cisco).
- Eighty-two percent of marketers of B2B (business-to-business) businesses affirm the popularity of video marketing to their content marketing strategy (Content Marketing Institute).
- Two-thirds of marketers see the video as the dominant trend in content marketing (iab).
- Fifty-two percent of marketers find videos the most effective means of creating brand awareness.
- Seventy percent of B2B marketers find video marketing as the most effective driver of conversions.
- Sixty-seven percent of marketers found video marketing a success (Digital Information World).
- Among businesses using video marketing, eighty-one percent realized increased sales while fifty-three percent

realized a reduction in support calls due to their 'How-to' products videos (OptinMonster).

- Eighty-three percent of businesses hold that video marketing gives them a positive ROI while Eighty-two percent feel the video is important to their marketing strategy. Already 63% of businesses have started using video content marketing (Wyzowl statistics)

- Ninety-six percent of B2B businesses are planning to use video marketing over the next twelve months.

- Seventy-five percent of executives watch work-related videos at least once a week. Sixty-five percent of them visit marketer's website after watching them. Thirty-nine percent of them call a marketer's vendor after watching the video (Forbes).

From these info statistics, you can see the important place of video marketing in an effective marketing strategy. Video marketing is the way to the present and future success.

Why video marketing has comparative advantage over other forms of advertising

There are many compelling reasons that give video marketing a comparative advantage to other forms of advertising. The following are just but a few:

1. **Video marketing can boost your site's SEO**

Quality and relevant video marketing content could greatly boost your site's SEO. It is easier to improve your business SEO value and boost conversion rate by adding video to your content offers, landing pages, and websites. This is evidenced by the fact that 65% of business executives visit a marketer's website after watching a branded video. This could also be true of other customers, though, at different percentages.

2. Video Marketing Can Explain Everything

The fact that most searches on YouTube are for explainer videos means that most users get more satisfaction from explainer videos than explainer text. A whopping 98% of video viewers have sought explainer videos just to learn more about a product or service. Those businesses that put explainer videos on their homepage claim it to be 83% effective. Of all businesses that use video marketing, 45% say that they have an explainer video on their home page.

3. Video increases sales and conversion

According to studies, seventy-four percent of viewers who watched explainer videos about a product ended up buying it. Again, adding a product video on your product page has been found to improve conversions by about eighty percent.

4. Video Encourages Social Shares

Social Videos are more likely to be shared than text and images. Studies have shown that they generate 1200% more shares than both text and images combined. This means that they have a wider reach. Seventy-six percent of social video consumers say that they are more likely to share branded videos with their friends if they are funny and entertaining.

5. Video content performs well on all devices

Knowing that 60% of YouTube videos and 90% of Twitter videos are watched on mobile devices, video content becomes the best option for content marketing across devices. Furthermore, 92% of mobile video viewers share their videos.

This is primarily due to the fact that video content is highly compatible across devices unlike blog and web content, which is highly dependent on the browser features and coding methods. It is hard to create web content that will retain the same quality features across devices.

6. Video Builds Trust

Videos, especially live videos build more trust than any other form of online content marketing. This is because people can see who is talking. They can relate to the body language and emotions. They can detect telling signs that determine whether someone is trustworthy or not. Generally, an untrustworthy person would not like to feature in videos, as this is too much of evidence to give. Thus, consumers gain more trust from video marketing than blog marketing. Studies show that 57% of consumers say that they gained more confidence in a product by watching videos.

7. Video Engages Even the Laziest Buyers

Many people are too lazy to read. However, even the laziest do love watching videos. This means video marketing can reach a much wider audience than a blog or text/image content could.

8. Video Shows Great ROI

Every businessperson's interest is to have a good return on investment (ROI). Eighty-three percent of businesses have found out that video marketing brings better returns on investment. With an increasing number of potential customers consuming more video content than TV content, this is obviously a greater and much cheaper way to optimize on ROI.

9. Google Loves Videos

It is no doubt that Google is the world's largest search engine and the king of internet content. If you want your content to be found and reach out to many, then, you have to comply with Google standards. You have to optimize your content for Google Search Engine. YouTube Search Engine, another Google product is the second largest search engine and the largest when it comes to video search.

Content that has video rank higher on Google SERP (Search Engine Results Page) than content without video. This shows the importance of using videos to market your content and products.

10.   Video content promotes brand recall

When it comes to branding, the main objective is to have people remember your product. Without the ability to recall, you have no brand. Studies have found out that 80% of viewers remember a video that they watched last month. This is a high rate of recall compared to text-based content at only 10%. Thus, using videos for purposes of brand recognition is critical. The more people recall a brand the more likely they are going to look for it while shopping.

11. Video marketing can help strengthen your brand message

You can use videos to create a brand persona. You can create a brand narrative that people can easily relate to. A mix of voice and content can greatly accentuate your brand identity.

12. Mobile Users love videos

Video content is the most consumed content on mobile phones. Ninety percent of customers watch videos on their mobile devices. The growth of mobile video doubles every year. Furthermore, smartphone video viewers are two times more likely to experience personal brand connection than TV viewers are, and 1.4 times more likely than Desktop viewers are.

DIFFERENT VIDEO MARKETING PLATFORMS

Video marketing is not just about hosting videos but also about using videos to reach your target market. While there are several great video-hosting platforms out there, our core interest here is about how that helps you to market.

The advantage of videos is that you can host them at one place and market them at another place via links. However, hybrid platforms (such as social video platforms) allow you to host and market at the same point. We will give a mention to some of the best video hosting platforms out there. Afterwards, we will focus on the marketing platforms.

Best video hosting platforms

When it comes to video hosting, you are spoilt for choice. The following are some of the leading video hosting platforms:

- YouTube
- Bits on the Run
- Vimeo PRO
- SproutVideo
- Dailymotion
- Brightcove

- Metacafe
- Wistia
- Vidyard
- Oculu
- Vimeo
- Vzaar
- Ooyala

These are just a few of the so many video hosting platforms that currently exist on the internet. So, how do you know the best?

To be able to determine which of them is best for you, you need to answer the following questions:

- What do you need from a platform?
- What kind of files do you have?
- How do you know which platform is best for your particular need?
- What kind of business problem are you solving with your product?
- What benefits have you realized?

Video Hosting on YouTube

YouTube is the most popular video hosting site. It is hybrid as it encompasses both hosting and social video marketing functions. It is also a search engine in its own regard. It is the second largest search engine after Google Search.

YouTube has great inbuilt tools that help you to host, market and monetize your videos. You can market and engage with your prospects. You can also present multiple videos to your audience thus boosting content absorption rate.

Integration:

Plenty of free tools (some of them are third-party tools) exist that you can use to boost your productivity while enhancing viewers' experience. Some of these tools include:

- SocialBlade
- VidIQ
- TubeBuddy
- Tubular Labs

You can also integrate with Gmail, Dropbox, Wistia, WordPress, Slack and many more utilities by using third-party integration tools such as Zapier.

We shall revisit YouTube under Social Video Marketing to explore more on its marketing features.

Video Hosting with Wistia

Wistia has a great hosting and analytics platform. It has a host of features geared towards customer support, sales, marketing, HR and recruitment among others.

The following are just but a few of its prominent features:

- Turnstile forms.
- Video heat-maps – These enable you to analyze viewing sessions of everyone who views your video. This helps you determine which sections they watched, re-watched or even jumped altogether.
- Chapters
- Password
- Email collectors
- Viewing Trends
- Call to Actions - Email collectors and Call to Actions features enable you to overlay interactive forms or text on your video. Just as you do on your blog, these enable you to sprinkle CTA's throughout your video.

Integration Capabilities:

You can easily integrate Wistia with major marketing automation platforms such as Zendesk, Marketo, Hubspot, Pardot etc. In addition, plenty of add-ons and extensions exist that you can use as Chrome and Gmail extensions.

Plenty of third-party add-ons exist that enable you to create, enhance or export your videos while they are hosted on the platform. These include Animoto, AirWich, GoAnimate, Reelcontent, Hapyak, among others.

Video Hosting With Vidyard

Vidyard is a great replacement for boring PowerPoint presentations. You can easily convert these slides into Vidyard videos and email them to your customers. Furthermore, you can customize these videos to include specialized details about your viewer such as company name, person's name, email, social network contact, etc.

Vidyard has plenty of features. Some of these features include:

- Interactive events
- A/B split testing
- Vidyard Studio
- Vidyard Live
- Personalized video

Interactive Events is a unique feature that replaces traditional text overlays and annotations. It overlays any JavaScript, HTML5 or CSS3 to create interactive elements such as product listings, dropdowns, and forms, among others.

Integration Capabilities

Vidyard boasts of a large number of integration options. These include Salesforce, Hubspot, Marketo, SnapApp, Eloqua, Mailchimp, Pardot, SalesFlot, and Adobe Act-on, among so many others. It also enables integration with email, maps, blog content, social platforms, and maps, among others.

Marketwise, Vidyard allows you to embed CTAs and track their performance. It also enables you to target leads, and close leads.

Video hosting with Vimeo Pro

Vimeo is a great choice for Filmmakers and Creatives. Its reputation in this regard came from it being the first platform to host HD video. It is great for professional high-resolution videos. It is highly optimized for speed across different devices.

Some of the great features of Vimeo Pro include:

- Customizable profile with cover video

- Unlimited bandwidth in the Vimeo player
- Time-saving video asset management tools
- Full SEO visibility
- Highly intuitive video analytics tools
- Fully embeddable and customizable HTML5 players
- Caption and subtitle creating tools
- Professional video management and workflow tools
- No adds before, after, or on top of your videos
- Up to 20GB of 4K Ultra HD video storage per week
- Upload, share and sell 360 videos
- High-quality HD encoding
- Support for galleries, albums, and video grouping
- Mobile video player support
- Multiple formats and sized download options for every video on its platform

Integration Capabilities:

Vimeo Pro is lazy when it comes to integration. It supports mainly Google Drive and Adobe. However, you can integrate with Zapier to extend its facility to include Gmail, Facebook, WordPress, Rave etc.

The only downside of Vimeo Pro is for lead generation and conversion. It may not be ideal for that purpose.

Social video marketing platforms

Social media has taken over the world of internet traffic. Social media networks consume a huge chunk of internet traffic. Thus, any serious marketer cannot ignore social media. This brings about the essence of social video marketing.

What is social video?

A social video is a type of video specifically created to be shared across social network platforms.

Why social videos are key to your marketing goals

The trend in social networks is towards social videos. More and more people are on social media to increasingly sharing social videos. The following are crucial indicators as to why social video is crucial to your marketing goals:

- **More social networks are creating native video infrastructure** – This demonstrates the growing value of social video to their users. Instagram, Twitter, and Snapchat have all embraced native infrastructure for social videos. YouTube and Vine are specifically tailored to social video. Periscope, Meerkat, and Facebook have live streaming social videos.

- **Social videos have great Return on Investment (ROI)** – Various statistics have shown that social videos have a great impact on consumers, resulting in a positive impact on businesses

- **Your competitors are already using social video** – You cannot ignore the fact that most businesses are leveraging the benefits of social videos. You cannot effectively compete with them if you are absent on this platform. That will grant them a competitive edge over you.

- **Social video has higher ability to connect with viewers** – Viewers easily connect with videos than they do with text. For example, on Twitter, you can only give 280 characters of text response. Yet, 30 seconds of video can deliver almost a million worth of words.

- **Social video appeals to the most important demographic (18 – 34 year-olds)** – This demographic consumes 90% of video content on the internet. It is flexible, adaptive and more responsive to marketing campaigns. It is also the largest demographic.

Where do social videos fit into your marketing plan?

It is definite that social videos can easily fit into your marketing strategy. How it does depends on your marketing plan and nature of the business. The following are some of the ways by which social videos fit into a general marketing strategy:

- **Brand Awareness** – It allows you to tell your brand story, thus creating awareness.

- **Employer branding** –It allows you to create a positive impression of your organizational culture.

- **Lead generation** - Reactions such as shares, likes, mentions, retweets, etc, enable you to unearth potential leads to target.

- **Call-to-action** - Annotations (clickable icons that appear on top of your video) on YouTube can help you compel your viewers to subscribe to your channel or direct viewers to a landing page on your website.

- **Customer engagement and support strategy** - Answering customer FAQ in a visual and personal way is possible using social video. It is a great way of answering how-to questions. Being sharable, it allows customers and your audience to share them with friends who could be having similar issues.

- **How-to product demos** – You can easily create a video-based how-to instructional manual for your customers.

This helps them to see practically how you are using your product to fix their problems.

Social video marketing platforms

It is no doubt that social media has the highest volume of internet traffic. This means video marketing platforms that are social-media-based are the best option when it comes to video marketing.

In this regard, you must consider the following top **social video marketing** platforms listed below. These are listed in order of importance:

- YouTube
- Instagram
- Snapchat
- Facebook
- Twitter
- Vine

EFFECTIVELY USING VIDEOS TO MARKET YOUR PRODUCTS AND SERVICES

There is no doubt that the future of digital marketing is video. Yet, just using videos does not necessarily guarantee you success. You must use it effectively in order to successfully market your products and services.

How to effectively use videos

Most businesses and marketers shun video marketing simply because they find themselves limited in their ability to use videos to market their products and services effectively.

The following steps can greatly help you to market your products and services using videos:

1. Prepare adequately

Adequate preparations will help you have an effective and coherent video marketing strategy. A great video marketing strategy will enable you to use videos to market your products and services effectively.

The following are some of the questions that you will need to answer in order to ascertain that you are adequately prepared:

What do you want to vlog about?

You have to decide on the topics you want to engage in with your audience. It could be about explanations, FAQs, tutorials or simply about your industry.

What Is Your Industry or Niche?

Your niche will not only determine the type of audience to engage, the platform to engage your audience on but also the kind of videos to make. You have to be well informed and passionate about your niche. If you are a marketer, you have to choose a niche that you are passionate about. This is what will drive your endeavor and draw you closer to your audience.

Who is Your Audience on YouTube?

There is no doubt that you would need a YouTube presence for your vlog. You need to determine your viewer persona. This will help you draw out an appropriate message and target them. This will also help you in shaping your topics.

What are Your Short-Term and Long-Term Vlogging Goals?

You have to establish your immediate, short-term and long-term goals of your vlogging. This will help you not only be specific about your targets, fine-tune your content, but also measure your performance.

Who is your vlogger?

Vlogging is not as easy as blogging. Thus, you would probably need a helping hand. Almost anyone can blog, but few can vlog. You have to determine carefully whether you can do it yourself or you need someone more appropriate to do it. You have to factor in the personality expected of your target audience.

Which name to use?

Your channel deserves a good name. You should choose a name that is attractive, interesting and easy to remember.

2. Make great marketing videos

A great video needs to be good both aesthetically and in content value. To achieve this:

Ensure high-quality content

When it comes to videos, quality matters a lot. A poor-quality video will do you more damage than good. While aesthetics can be appealing, the message too should be presented in an inspiring, intriguing, funny and entertaining manner. Also, the message should deliver value not only to your viewers but also to your brand.

Make a set (series) in advance

The best way to attract a following and build a community is to deliver content consistently. Just one video is not enough to enable you to build a community. This means that you will keep on releasing new videos to keep feeding your community and increase their appetite for more.

Edit your videos

Before publishing your videos, make sure that you edit them thoroughly for aesthetics, content value, and even presentation. You will never miss something requiring improvement. Share with your friends and let them give their input and perspective.

3. Publish your videos

Once you are satisfied with your editing standard, release your videos one by one as per schedule. You can start with a longer interval for a start and keep on shortening intervals as your community grows and you reach a point where you can release a video daily.

Post videos related videos to a well-performing video

If one video performs well, post another under it as part of your response. This way, you are using the popular video to market your other video.

Embed videos on your blog and website

Once you publish your video on YouTube, you will get embed codes. Use these codes to embed your video on your blog and website. This way, you not only continue the conversation on your blog/website but also increase the web's SEO performance. You also boost the experience of your blog readers.

Post your video on social media

Post your video on social media to increase conversation. However, not all YouTube videos are ideal for social media. You may need to customize your videos so that they are hosted natively on respective social media. Videos hosted natively on social media tend to have higher engagement and conversion rates compared to those that are not. Nonetheless, if you cannot manage to do it natively, it is still better to post your YouTube videos on social media than provide no video at all.

4. Promote your vlog

Videos consume more time and resources than blogs. Thus, it is good to maximize on their returns. It is worth promoting them so that they receive the widest reach possible and have the widest impact. You can advertise them through Pay-per-Click (PPC) model. PPC is relatively cheap and most likely cheaper than the opportunity cost of not reaching out to the potential audience.

5. Build your vlog community

In the long-term, it will cost less in terms of advertisement and impact more in terms of conversions when you have a community around your vlog. As we have seen, your audience can easily market for you free of charge and in a more impactful way than you would if you were to advertise. Thus, building a community is not only cost-effective but also more profitable.

To build your community, you need to:

Vlog consistently

Information is consumed more frequently than food. It creates more hunger than food and more thirst than water. Consumers of your information would not want you to starve them. Thus, the best way to make them not go elsewhere is to feed them with quality and satisfying information consistently. You must blog frequently and consistently so that, just as you know the time you expect your breakfast, lunch, and dinner, they too know the time they expect their knowledge-food (video content).

Engage your audience

You build your community when you let them be actively involved. Respond to their questions and comments. Ask them for feedback. This way, they will feel appreciated, engaged, and entertained.

6. Become YouTube Partner

Becoming a YouTube Partner has a great advantage in your video marketing endeavor. This is especially crucial when you want to monetize your vlogs. When you become a YouTube Partner, you can allow YouTube to display ads on your videos (that is, if you desire to monetize your videos). You also get to be ranked better in search results.

Strategies to use video in your marketing

- **Use an editorial calendar** – Editorial calendar will help you plan, organize and schedule your videos so that you become more consistent and align yourself with your business goals.

- **Upload videos natively to social media** – Videos that are natively posted on social media perform better than those that are shared directly from YouTube.
- **Use videos to share your brand story** – Visualizing your brand story brings connecting with your viewers as they are able to experience your passion and zeal in serving your market
- **Include videos in your email marketing** – Emails with videos in them tend to achieve a more positive response than text emails. Make sure that you include the word 'video' in your email's subject line so that the readers are aware that there is a video in the email. They will give it more priority than other emails in the inbox.
- **Curate your popular blog posts into video content to extend your reach** – Instead of popular blog posts lying idle on your website, repurpose them as video content to increase their utility.
- **Create videos for each product** – Each product should stand on its own. Not all products appeal to the same audience. Demonstrate its features, specs, benefits, and usage.
- **Take advantage of live video** – Live video boosts engagement. They help you to connect deeper with your followers. Take advantage of Periscope, Instagram Stories, and Facebook Live. You can use live streaming to

announce breaking news, invite them to your next event or informing them of a new blog post. You can also use live video to announce great product offers.

DRIVING TRAFFIC TO YOUR WEBSITES WITH VIDEOS

Driving traffic to your websites with videos is the ultimate aim of most video marketing campaigns. Unless you are in the business of selling videos as a product or receiving advertising revenue via videos, you are more likely going to want to drive traffic from your video source to your website's landing pages or product pages.

Why use video to drive traffic to your websites?

As highlighted by our established findings and info statistics in our previous sections, we found out that video content receives more traffic than text content and this continues to grow such that, by 2019, it is anticipated that 80% of web traffic will be generated by videos. This is a compelling reason as to why you ought to tap into videos as a source of traffic to your websites.

Ways to drive traffic to your website

The following are some of the ways by which you can use your videos to drive traffic to your website:

1. Annotations

Annotation is the best place to put a clear and targeted call to action (CTA). This should inform viewers exactly what they expect should they click on the provided link.

However, you must not forget that annotations do no work on mobile devices. Thus, you will also need to incorporate your CTA elsewhere to target mobile users. Descriptions become the best location to target them.

Furthermore, do not forget that you must verify your ownership of that particular website domain with YouTube before you can link it in your annotations.

To be able to use annotations:

- Verify your YouTube account (YouTube.com/verify). YouTube will seek confirmation via your mobile phone.
- Once your YouTube account is verified, you can go to Advanced channel settings and add your website domain under "Associated Websites". The domain will be added but it will remain pending until you verify it.
- You can verify your domain through various methods provided by Google. These include adding a tag to your

site's homepage, uploading a blank HTML file to your site's home folder, or through Google Analytics or Web Master's Tools.

- Upon verification, you will see a green dot next to Advanced channel settings. You will also see a drop-down option with your normal annotations labeled "Associated Website" which allows you to link any URL (e.g. landing page, product page, etc) to that domain.

2. Descriptions

Descriptions are the best place to put links to videos that appeal to both mobile and non-mobile video viewers. Since only the first three lines appear on the video before the "Show More" truncation, your links should appear within the first three lines, preferably the second line. Use the first line to direct viewers to click on the link provided on the second line. For example, "Find more about my products here" can be on the first line and relevant link to your product page can be on the subsequent line. You must not forget to precede "http://" to your URL link. Otherwise, it will not be clickable.

While annotations are not visible on mobile devices, descriptions are not visible on embedded players (such as embeds on your websites). Thus, if you want people to click on your links from embeds; you must take advantage of other places such as End Cards or CTA overlays.

End cards

End Cards, as the name suggest, appear at the end of a video. This is an extra opportunity to interact with your audience beyond the video. You can provide interactive annotations on the End Cards or simply provide your web links.

CTA Overlay links

CTA overlay is a small rectangular box that is at times displayed in a little "shutter box" at the bottom on the left side of a video. This appears only when you choose to promote your YouTube video using AdWords for TrueView/Video.

The advantage of CTA overlays is that they are also displayed on other devices.

How to make a CTA overlay:

1. Setup AdWords for video campaign (make it paused as an active one will be filled by YouTube ads instead)
2. Go to Videos tab and Click the "+" icon box next to "Add call-to-action overlay"
3. Enter your CTA text

The CTA text can comprise of the following:

- A headline
- Display URL (should be short)
- Destination URL (can be long)
- Optional image

If you want the CTA overlay to reflect on mobile, you must activate it. It does not appear by default.

Talent CTAs

People love following new talents. Thus, you can take advantage of a talented artists or influencer to call your CTA on the End Card. Alternatively; you can also let the artist do that within the video itself. This will not only prove the authenticity of your CTA but also inspire action from your audience.

AFFILIATE MARKETING WITH VIDEO MARKETING

Affiliate marketing is one of the most prominent forms of commission-based marketing on the internet today. Millions of products are sold on the internet through thousands of affiliate marketers. Due to the increasing prominence of video content and vlogging, affiliate marketing has also been spreading from its traditional domain in blogs to vlogs. This has brought forth affiliate video marketing.

What is Affiliate Video Marketing?

Affiliate video marketing is a commission-based marketing fronted by affiliates who create videos to promote or endorse your products and services. Their reward is based on the sales made by the affiliate's marketing endeavor.

What Can Affiliate Marketing Do for You?

Affiliate marketing does a lot. This is why it is loved by most businesses.

The following are some of the things that affiliate video marketing can do for you:

- **Free up your time** – As a businessperson, you need plenty of time to focus on creative endeavors. Using affiliates can free up a lot of your time that you would have otherwise spent on creating and marketing videos. An affiliate will create videos using instructions provided by you and carry out video marketing effort on your behalf.

- **Reduce Marketing Costs** – Affiliate marketers earn a commission based on results (that is, successful sales). This means that you do not have to spend upfront nor incur costs that cannot be financed by your sales. This helps you to save on marketing budget and relocate the savings to other needy areas.

- **Gain larger audience** – Every affiliate marketer has their own YouTube account and probably other social video accounts. This means that your product videos will get more exposure and you will get a larger audience than you would have achieved on your own. Furthermore, you can have as many affiliates as possible since you are not constrained by upfront payment or non-sale related payments.

- **Increase traffic to your website** – Larger audience means more potential for traffic flows to your website.

- **Unique voices** – Every voice appeals to its audience. Having more unique voices means catering to different kinds of audiences. You can achieve this through affiliates.

How to promote affiliate products through YouTube video

The following steps will help you to market your affiliate products through YouTube successfully:

1. **Find an affiliate product you can promote** - Clickbank, Commission Junction, and Amazon Associates are some of the great places to find affiliate products to promote.
2. **Decide on the type of video you are going to create** – How-to videos are the best when it comes to affiliate video marketing. Nonetheless, you can introduce different types of videos so long as they relate to the product and are relevant.
3. **Create the Video** – You can create a video on your own. However, if you do not have the skills, equipment or time, you can outsource video creation to a freelancer. Fiverr and Upwork are great places to find professional freelancers to create videos on your behalf.

4. **Add a clickable affiliate link to the video** – After all, you want to sell your product. Affiliate links are the core reason for your video. Put your affiliate link at a strategic point in your video. Knowing that a good number of audience members do not finish watching videos, take advantage of the first 30 seconds to place your Call-to-Action inside your annotation. You also need to put your affiliate link within the first 25 characters of your description as only the first 27 characters are shown in the video while the rest is truncated as 'more info'. Very few watchers will click on 'more info'.

5. **Promote your affiliate video** – After adding your clickable link, you can now promote your affiliate video on YouTube, social media, website and blog.

How Does Payout Work?

The respective affiliate network tracks every affiliate link provided. Every time someone clicks on the affiliate link, this triggers a cookie to be stored on the person's device thus tracking what he or she purchases and when the purchase is done. These purchases are registered in the affiliate network's database for purposes of computing the affiliate's commission payout. Of particular benefit to affiliates is that most cookies simply record purchases from a particular website, thus, the affiliate will still earn even if a buyer clicks on other products on the website other than those the affiliate was promoting.

What are the Commission Rates?

Commission rates vary from product to product. Every brand has its own commission rate. For example, Amazon has 5% payout on some products and 10% payout on others. Some sellers provide even up to 50% payout. It all depends on the owner's marketing strategy. If a business owner realizes that an affiliate sells products that the business would not have otherwise sold on its own, then, it will give more incentives to affiliates in terms of higher commission.

BLOGGING WITH VIDEO MARKETING

Though vlogging is gaining more at the expense of blogging, blogging is still going to be with us for a long time to come. This is primarily due to the ease with which one can create a blog compared to a vlog. In addition, the cost of preparing a blog is still far lower than that of preparing a vlog. Internet speeds and internet costs, though rapidly dropping down, are still prohibitive to many netizens, especially in the developing world.

The great thing about blogs is that they are easy to integrate with videos. You simply need to embed your video in a blog. They do have some sort of symbiotic relationship as they increase each other's consumption. Furthermore, they help in driving traffic to each other as they promote each other's SEO.

How to determine whether vlogging is ideal for you

If you possess the following seven qualities, then Vlogging is right for you:

- You enjoy planning and self-commitment
- You enjoy speaking to a camera
- You are confident in freely and publicly expressing your thoughts
- You enjoy editing videos

- You love learning new ways of doing things
- You love interacting with people and appreciate your engagement with them
- You enjoy social media presence

How to enable vlogs to work for your blogs

The following are the steps you will need to take to create a vlog for your blog:

1. Create your video script
2. Shoot your video
3. Upload your vlog file to YouTube
4. Create and post relevant blog
5. Get the video embed code
6. Embed your video code at the right place in your blog post
7. Publish your blog post
8. Test your embedded code
9. Share your blog post on social media

How to boost viewership on your vlog

Getting more viewers on your YouTube channel simply means you have a greater traffic to direct to your blog. The following are some of the ways that can help you gain more viewers for your YouTube channel:

- Consistently create and post high-quality videos on your YouTube channel
- Use attractive and appealing video titles to impress viewers
- Give priority to community building as opposed to quick sales
- Partner with other vloggers in collaborative efforts
- Be an active blogger and share your updates on both your blog and vlog
- Become a guest blogger/vlogger on other people's accounts
- Leverage social media to drive more traffic to your vlogs
- Vlog passionately and keep doing it

How to build community on your channel

The greater the community around your channel, the more certain the source of traffic to your blog.

- Select an attractive name for your channel's community
- Appreciate your Vlog community
- Consistently interact and engage with your followers
- Request feedback, ideas, and topics from your followers

- Expose your vlogs on social media to establish a dominant presence

How to make your commenting section more active and productive

- Respond to questions from viewers
- Start and boost discussions in the commenting section
- Offer challenging questions to viewers as you conclude your video
- Explore avenues to expose your audience to greater levels of involvement
- Request viewers to elicit ideas and opinions on what they would expect in the next video
- Proudly display best comments at the conclusion of your videos

How to inspire a loyal following on your vlog channel

- Be consistent in providing quality, relevant, informative and entertaining videos
- Give your channel a unique personality
- Leverage blogging
- Engage influencers through collaborative effort

- Find new creative ways to engage your audience – it could be contests, prizes on regular commentators, etc.
- Find ways to inspire your followers to share your videos
- Build a social media community for your vlog channel
- Express passion for your vlog and appreciation for your fans

How to brand your vlog channel

- Have an interesting and catchy channel name
- Have a simple, memorable and unique logo for your channel brand
- Share your brand logo on social media
- Make sure your video content is branded as per your channel, blog, website, and products e.g. in terms of colors, fonts, etc.
- Engage your audience about your brand features and why they inspire you
- Create an interesting narrative about your brand choice

Making your new YouTube channel a great success

- Define your "success" as part of your strategic goal
- Define your viewer persona that you ought to target
- Express passion in all your vlogging endeavors
- Show a positive attitude to your audience
- Collaborate and network with others in the vlogosphere

How to boost personal connection with your vlog channel

- Be humane
- Interact live with your audience
- Engage your audience on a personal level
- Be natural
- Respond to comments with a personal touch
- Communicate in a less formal language
- Tease your audience with tricky and interesting questions

INCREASE YOUR CHANCES OF MAKING VIRAL VIDEO

Virality has become a buzzword in internet marketing, and more so, with the advent of social media. On Facebook, the volume of shares determines virality. On Twitter, the volume of retweets determines virality. Traditionally, virality has been associated with text-based and image-based posts and tweets. However, with video content increasingly playing a more assertive role, we cannot ignore the viral video.

What is a viral video?

A viral video is one that causes a sudden reaction, leading to it being spread far and wide, both online and offline. Such reactions include likes, follows, mentions, sharing, retweets etc.

A viral video helps to boost brand visibility and recognition – and if positive, brand acceptance. It can also help to create potential leads and motivate buy decision.

Key ingredients of a viral video

The following are key ingredients of a viral video:

1. **Social currency**

   It is human nature to validate one's social standing. Thus, people will be more inclined to share content that makes them feel knowledgeable and smart. The content should be such as to make them feel the same.

2. **Social Motivation**

   There are certain social motivations that make them desire to share with others. The same applies to video content. The following are some of the common social motivations that would drive people to share videos with others:

   - Associate oneself with a great idea
   - Share first-hand information
   - Trigger a topic for discussion
   - Promote a good cause
   - Gauge friends' responses
   - Demonstrate thought leadership and authority
   - Provide useful solution
   - Boost engagement and interactions offline
   - Connect with friends about shared interest or passion
   - Further discussion on the current trend or event

Thus, to create a viral video, you should make it capable of triggering some or most of these social motivations.

3. Emotion

Emotional content is content which triggers a strong emotional reaction in the viewer. When it comes to social media, this reaction will be expressed in terms of likes, mentions, shares, retweets, etc, depending on the social media platform.

Emotional content is that content that connects with the viewer at the heart level. It is inspiring, compelling, authentic, and at times, surprising and shocking.

4. Practical value

People react to content that proves a superior solution to their needs and those of others. The practical value could include budget cutting, time-saving, ease of availability, convenience, benefit, etc.

5. Storytelling

People love listening to captivating narratives. Create a video that associates your brand or blends it with a compelling narrative. This way, people will remember it and will find something in it worth sharing.

How to Create Content That Goes Viral

Creating content that goes viral is about blending the viral ingredients, optimizing the blend, packaging the blend into a viral product and delivering it to the viral trigger.

The high-arousal emotional trigger is what will spread the video out there like wildfire. The following are the powerful high-arousal triggers that you need to incorporate into your video marketing campaign:

- **Joy** – People have so many things that dampen their spirits. They would cherish anything that brightens up their moods and etches out a smile on their face. Videos that evoke positive feelings will help them spread their joy. Yes, no one enjoys it alone. It has to be with someone else.

- **Affection** – People need to feel loved, cared for and emotionally pampered. Bring affection to your product, even if it is not applicable to such areas. Just create a narrative of affection and blend your product's application towards enhancing it.

- **Trust** – Trust is the key ingredient that brings about customer loyalty and builds a community of followers. Create videos that trigger an impression of trust. Bring out a narration of how you helped to solve customers' challenges or addressed their worries and concerns. Those who share the same challenges, worries or concerns will find you and your brand trustworthy. Incorporating this as part of testimonials can be a great rallying point.

- **Pride** – Humans are egoistic by nature. They would want to enjoy bragging rights. Unfortunately, most advertisers have used big names in their adverts such as Oscar stars, sports stars, supermodels, etc, that make ordinary viewers feel exasperated, inferior, and beyond reach. Instead, create a video that makes everyone feel a hero. A video that ignites a sense of vigor, boosts self-esteem and ignite conversations that center on each other's inner-power/inner-strength rather than being spectators of those beyond them.

- **Funny and Amusing** – People want to laugh. Feel cheerful and happy. Funny videos provide these. People hardly forget what makes them laugh. A video that is amusing will be remembered for long. Furthermore, when it is shared, even if one forgets, someone else will remind him. Thus, the memory expands beyond an individual into a community. Amusing videos are greatly shared. The funnier is the video the more the shares. However, do not substitute your brand for amusement. Find a way to blend and balance. What would be the use if a video goes viral, without benefiting your brand?

- **Surprise** – You need to provide in your video something unexpected. This could be a new feature, a new discovery in your industry, a new application of your product, a new fact, a new mode of delivery, etc. it could also be a surprise offer. Just blend it with other emotional triggers to have maximum impact.

- **Fear** – Fear is an extremely powerful emotion. Insurance companies, emergency rescue companies, security companies and even religious institutions take advantage of people's fears to market their products/services. Examples of fears that you can consider include; fear of losing out a great bonus/discount/offer, fear of missing a deadline, fear of risk, fear of failure, etc. Just look out for common fears associated with your niche and find ways to incorporate into your video.

- **Uncertainty** – Try to disturb the comfort zones. Trigger some restlessness. Ruffle feathers. This way, you can make people snap out of your competitor's nest. It could be about debunking a certain myth or a certain aspect that makes people glued to your competitor's products. It could be about challenging a long-held belief (maybe about the efficacy of a certain key ingredient), etc. Just do not make yourself appear to directly target your competitor. Make it subtle.

OTHER WAYS TO USE VIDEO MARKETING

You can use video marketing in many other ways. The following are some of the ways:

Personal brand identity – Just as you market your business, you too can also market yourself as a brand. This is what artists do. As a professional marketer or as a professional in other fields, it is important to create a great personal image revolving around your profession and core competencies. This is a great deal especially when you want to establish yourself as a consultant in a particular field.

Thought leadership – Thought leadership has become a high-value personal brand. It is no longer a preserve of greatly influential people such as former presidents, former heads of international organizations, great entrepreneurs, and successful CEOs. You too can become a thought leader in your particular field/niche. You can create a niche to specialize in and create leading thoughts about it. Video marketing can help you advance your thought leadership and gain a loyal audience around your thoughts.

Public Relations – Public relations is a function of strategic communication. Video marketing can help communicate to your target audience (publics) in such a manner that triggers an intended perception about you and/or your brand.

Testimonials – Testimonials are great when it comes to building trust. You can have testimonials about your personal brand or business brand. Testimonials are independent third-party opinions. You can encourage people to give their own testimonies through video interviews by a journalist.

Key staff profiles – If you own a business, it is good for your potential customers to know who your key staff is and how they contribute to their own personal experience with your product that they consume. This helps them have more confidence in your competence as a solution provider to their needs.

Breakthrough Announcements – There are times when you make a breakthrough, either in your personal life (for personal branding) or as a business (product brand). Demonstrating these breakthroughs is the best way to inspire potential customers and boost appetite of the already existing customers.

CONCLUSION

Thank you for acquiring and reading this book.

This book guides you on how to sharpen your brand visibility, boost customer loyalty and increase sales using videos.

It is my hope that information provided in this book has inspired you to start creating videos to market your business. It is also my sincere hope that you have shared information about this book with others so that they too can have a copy that will guide them on how to propel their businesses through video marketing.

Good luck!

www.ingramcontent.com/pod-product-compliance
Lightning Source LLC
Chambersburg PA
CBHW070856070326
40690CB00009B/1861